Streets of Liverpool

Martin Jenkins and Charles Roberts

Ian Allan
PUBLISHING

Front cover: For many years the hub of Liverpool's local transport network centred on George's Pier Head, the official name for the large open area in front of the city's three waterfront buildings, now a World Heritage Site. Liverpool had possessed one of the most progressive tramways in the country, with many modern cars. In 1955 the Pier Head was a bustling mixture of trams, buses and cars, not forgetting the people — Liverpudlians themselves, as well as those from 'over the water' (the Wirral) who travelled over by ferry for work, shopping or entertainment. All are shown in this scene. 'Liner' tram No 950 bides its time before departing for Pagemoss on route 10B. An Austin FX3 taxicab drops off a passenger. Buses wait on the site of two former tramway loops, already well on their way to eradicating trams from the streets of Liverpool. *J. B. C. McCann*

Previous page: Old Haymarket in the late 1960s, when it was still serving as a terminus for Liverpool Corporation and Ribble buses. The Municipal Building clock tower stands proudly above all the buildings around it, while the Liver Birds peer imperiously above the skyline. Tunnel tolls were still being collected at both ends of the Mersey Tunnel; nowadays all payment is made on the Wirral side. *Mike Mercer*

This book is dedicated to the memory of John McCann, who recorded so many wonderful streetscapes in and around the city.

First published 2007

ISBN (10) 0 7110 3198 3
ISBN (13) 978 0 7110 3198 2

© Ian Allan Publishing 2007

Published by Ian Allan Publishing

an imprint of Ian Allan Publishing Ltd, Hersham, Surrey, KT12 4RG
Printed in England by Ian Allan Printing Ltd, Hersham, Surrey, KT12 4RG

Code: 0708/B1

Visit the Ian Allan Publishing website at www.ianallanpublishing.com

Introduction

The year 2007 marks Liverpool's 800th anniversary as a borough, the 110th anniversary of the Corporation's assuming responsibility for its public transport and the 50th anniversary of the end of the trams.

Known as the city of ships (city status having been achieved in 1880), Liverpool owed its commercial pre-eminence to the impact of the Industrial Revolution and to its location on the east bank of the Mersey. The coming of the canals and railways opened up a giant manufacturing hinterland, establishing Liverpool as one of the world's major trading centres. From the opening of the first dock in 1715 expansion continued until completion of the deep-water Gladstone system in 1927.

From the 1840s the city was home to large numbers of Welsh, Scots and Irish, some sections of the city being divided along bitter sectarian lines. There were also significant Jewish and Chinese communities. To serve its burgeoning population a web of road and rail routes linked the city centre with the densely populated inner suburbs as well as more prosperous residential areas. Growing prosperity led to construction of many impressive civic and public buildings as well as fine residences for the merchant classes. In contrast, thousands existed in sub-standard dwellings, often in close proximity to the labour-intensive docks and warehouses. Such 'slum' areas would gradually be demolished, and in the 1920s and '30s some fine garden suburbs were built, to be followed after World War 2 by tower blocks and out-of-town estates.

For transport enthusiasts Liverpool has always had much to offer. In the late 1940s the river was home to every kind of vessel from ocean-going liners and warships to coasters and tramp steamers. Regular sailings left Prince's Landing Stage for most parts of the globe as well as for Ireland, the Isle of Man and, in the summer months, North Wales. Birkenhead Corporation ferry boats operated to and from Woodside, whilst those of Wallasey Corporation ran to and from Seacombe as well as New Brighton during the season. The city's three main stations (Exchange, Lime Street and Central) echoed to the sounds of steam, whilst goods trains worked to and from the docks. Electric trains from Exchange also served Ormskirk and Southport, while those from Central (Low Level) ran to points on the Wirral by way of a under-river or sub-fluvian tunnel. The Queensway road tunnel, opened in 1934, was still regarded as a wonder of the modern age, but by the mid-1950s the growth in car ownership, especially on the Wirral side, was causing severe rush-hour congestion as long queues formed around the tunnel approaches. Heavy traffic was also experienced in the vicinity of the docks, with their slow-moving lines of horse-drawn drays, lorries, steam 'waggons' and little shunting locomotives, while perched above was the Liverpool Overhead Railway.

The streets of Liverpool saw major changes during the period covered by this book. The unique Overhead Railway ran for the last time on 30 December 1956, following which the once-familiar structure was torn down, while on 14 September 1957 the Corporation completed its tram-replacement programme, commenced in 1948.

The trams had first arrived in the shape of company-owned horse cars in 1869, an earlier, short-lived, experimental line (opened in 1861) having proved unsuccessful. Liverpool Corporation acquired the tramway company in 1897 and set about electrification, rapidly expanding the system to provide cheap transport for residents of the growing suburban hinterland. Lines fanned out from the Pier Head to serve the northern, eastern and southern suburbs. Many routes encountered steep gradients, while narrow streets meant interlaced, single-track or one-way working. The most distinctive feature of the outer-suburban street scene was the miles of 'grass tracks' flanked by privet hedges — tramway reservations laid mostly in the centre of well-designed dual carriageways built to serve garden estates

with quality municipal housing. Construction of reserved track spanned 30 years, the last section opening in 1944 to serve the Royal Ordnance Factory at Kirkby. Liverpudlians benefited from one of the most progressive tramways in the country with its 97 miles of route, of which four miles were operated by Liverpool but owned by Bootle Corporation.

Modern designs of tram had begun to enter service in the late 1920s, to be followed in the 1930s by hundreds of new cars built at the Corporation's Edge Lane works. These included the well-known bogie 'Streamliners' and the more economic four-wheelers known as 'Baby Grands'. Red (crimson lake) and cream until 1933, the trams had then appeared in a new livery of olive-green and cream, earning them the nickname 'Green Goddesses' after a popular film of the time.

Although exciting plans existed for further tramway development postwar, the Transport Committee opted instead for buses. As a result the war-weary network of 191 miles of track and 744 trams was wiped out between 1948 and 1957, the 'modernists' having argued that tramway retention would hamper road-improvement schemes, especially in the congested central area. Aiming to overcome this congestion, the city

Previous page: The rich mix of architectural styles in Liverpool city centre is summed up by this picture taken from the St John's Precinct Beacon tower (the shadow of which can be seen bottom right) in the direction of Old Haymarket. The neo-classical design of the Museum and Central Technical School contrasts with the 1930s flats and the tower blocks of the 1960s and '70s, while cutting a swathe through the scene are the two Churchill Way flyovers. *Mike Mercer*

planners implemented numerous traffic-management schemes. From the mid-1960s inner-city streets disappeared, dual carriageways and flyovers were built, ever more buildings were demolished, and controversial one-way systems were introduced. From the mid-1970s many once-busy thoroughfares, notably Church Street and Parker Street, were also pedestrianised, with the result that long-established transport routes were altered, usually to the public's disadvantage. At the time of writing the city centre is again undergoing major redevelopment. The area around Paradise Street, redeveloped only 40 years ago following extensive bomb damage, will become the Liverpool One shopping complex, but advanced plans for a modern light-rail system linking the central area with key suburbs have been thwarted by a lack of Government funding.

Until 1969 local bus services were provided by Liverpool Corporation, the Crosville and Ribble companies operating the longer routes. A network of joint Corporation/Ribble routes served large parts of Bootle and Litherland. Added to the mix were buses from St Helens and Wigan Corporations and Lancashire United Transport; their vehicles appeared on a handful of routes including one lengthy service worked by no fewer than four operators.

Liverpool Corporation had started operating buses in 1911 following purchase of a small undertaking in Woolton. Gradually other routes were opened, most being feeders to the trams, but, with demands for through routeing into the city centre, buses reached the Pier Head in 1928. At the outbreak of World War 2 there were just 158 buses. However, wartime demand led to the arrival of second-hand vehicles and other previously unfamiliar types. Between 1946 and 1951 some 500 new double-deckers entered service, mostly as tram replacements. The majority were either AEC Regents or Leyland Titan PD2s, but there were a few Daimlers and Crossleys. Bodywork was provided by a variety of manufacturers, many being finished off at the Corporation's Edge Lane works. Experiments in the late 1950s with larger, higher-capacity vehicles led to the purchase of 380 rear-engined Leyland Atlanteans. In the late 1960s moves towards one-man operation (OMO) produced orders for Leyland Panther and Bristol RE single-deckers, these appearing in a reversed livery of cream with green window surrounds. On 1 December 1969 the fleets of Birkenhead, Liverpool and Wallasey Corporations were merged to form the Merseyside Passenger Transport Executive. In Liverpool the fleet remained in the familiar dark green and cream, although the opening in 1971 of the second Mersey road tunnel and the introduction of 'Cross River Express' routes brought blue-and-cream Wirral Division buses daily into the city.

Above: Shopping done, it's time to catch a bus home. Lord Street was characterised by a line of bus and (until 1957) tram stops at which shoppers and city-centre workers queued in polite fashion for their particular route. An early-postwar AEC Regent fills up on route 9C while those still waiting look anxiously towards the Victoria Monument to see their bus appearing over the hill. *G. H. Hesketh*

A photographic journey around the city, *Streets of Liverpool* starts in the central area before venturing out to the northern, eastern and southern suburbs. The pictures, ranging from the late 1930s to the early 1970s, reveal how the city and its transport changed in the intervening years. We hope this varied selection will revive memories for those who were around at the time and provide others with an insight into how the city used to be in the not-too-distant past.

Martin Jenkins
Walton-on-Thames, Surrey

Charles Roberts
Upton, Wirral
July 2007

Acknowledgements

The authors would especially like to thank Mair and Andy McCann, for the loan of slides taken by John McCann, Martin Hesketh, for slides taken by G. H. Hesketh, and Bill Barlow, Jonathan Cadwallader, Tony Gahan, Gareth Jenkins, Bruce Maund, Ian Parry and Tony Thomas, for their invaluable assistance with the captions. Other photographs are reproduced courtesy of the Leeds Transport Historical Society, the Light Rail Transit Association (London Region), Photobus (special gratitude being owed to the late Arnold Richardson) and Online Transport Archive (OTA), of which both authors are trustees (and to which their fees for this book are being donated). Established in 2000 to ensure that collections of transport slides, negatives and cine films are secured for posterity, OTA may be contacted via Ian Allan Publishing at the address given on page 2.

Bibliography

In compiling this book the authors have drawn on a number of publications, most notably *Liverpool Transport* (Vols 1-5) by J. B. Horne and T. B. Maund (LRTL/TPC, 1975-91), *A Nostalgic Look at Liverpool Trams* by Steve Palmer and Brian Martin (Silver Link, 1996), *Liverpool — it all came tumbling down* by Freddy O'Connor (Brunswick Press, 1986), *Liverpool's Railways* by Paul Anderson (Irwell Press, 1996), *Liverpool's Buses* by Paul Kelly (TPC, 1986), *Seventeen Stations to Dingle* by John W. Gahan (Countyvise / Avon Anglia, 1982) and *Liverpolitania* by Peter Howell-Williams (Merseyside Civic Society, 1971).

Above: Fifty years after its closure, the iconic Liverpool Overhead Railway is still sadly missed. Opened in 1893, it provided a fast, efficient means of moving large numbers of workers along the dock system. The Liver Building, the Cunard Building and the Mersey Tunnel ventilation shaft provide continuity, but everything in the foreground has gradually been swept away to accommodate the Strand/Goree dual carriageway. *Ray DeGroote*

Left: Among the many dockland buildings to have disappeared were two giant grain silos which towered above Sefton Street. The older brick structure (1906) was connected by a high-level bridge to the newer concrete one (1936). Serving the nearby docks had been Brunswick Dock station on the LOR. Also in this vicinity was a large railway goods yard with connections to the MDHB rail network. The low-level transit sheds were on the river side of the dock estate wall. Seen on LOR-replacement route 1, A544 (HKF 820) was from a batch of 100 AEC Regent IIIs of 1948/9 with narrow, somewhat austere Weymann bodywork completed at Edge Lane. They were withdrawn between 1962 and 1968. Retired in 1967, A544 was one of 25 of the batch with preselective gearboxes. Today it forms part of the collection of vintage vehicles housed at the Wirral Bus & Tram Museum in Taylor Street, Birkenhead. *H. B. Christiansen*

Left: Pier Head bus station and the river, seen from the Atlantic Tower Hotel on the corner of Chapel Street and the Dock Road. Dominating the scene is the largest of the three waterfront buildings, the one-time headquarters of the Royal Liver Friendly Society, dating from 1911. With its two 300ft towers each capped by effigies of the mythical Liver bird, this multi-storeyed reinforced concrete building designed by Aubrey Thomas has been described as Britain's first 'skyscraper'. For decades the Liver Birds have looked down onto a bustling river. However, by the time this view was recorded in the mid-1970s the Mersey was much quieter; the last passenger liners had sailed from Prince's Landing Stage, and only the Seacombe and Woodside ferries and the Isle of Man ferries still departed from George's Landing Stage. On the right of the picture is the floating roadway which had carried traffic to and from the half-mile-long floating landing stage. The purpose-built Pier Head bus station had opened in 1965, the variety of vehicles and the imposing architectural backdrop making it a prime location for photographers. *A. E. Jones*

Right: Dominating this 1949 view are the Cunard Building (1914) and the Mersey Docks & Harbour Board building (1907), which, together with the Royal Liver Building, stand on the site of the filled-in George's Dock (1761). During the tramway era the terminal was redesigned several times; after 1921 it comprised three large, interlinked loops (north, centre and south). Seen waiting to depart from the north loop are four cars built by the Corporation during the 1930s: on the inner track is No 779, one of 12 bogie cars dating from 1933; next is one of 85 domed-roof cars (1933-6) and finally one of 163 bogie 'Streamliners' (1936/7). On the outer track is No 288, one of the 100 four-wheel 'Baby Grands' (1938-42). The wartime legacy is much in evidence: one tram wears the 'dirty' green-grey livery applied to many buses and trams, an air-raid shelter can be seen in front of the Liver Building, while the Dock Board offices are under repair. When this loop was abandoned in January 1951 several tram routes were relocated to the two remaining loops. *C. Carter*

Right: Until absorbed into the new bus station in 1965 the old loop formed part of a turning-circle for buses. Seen on tram-replacement route 17D, L51 (NKD 651) was one of a batch of 60 8ft-wide Leyland PD2/12s with 56-seat Weymann bodywork, delivered during 1953/4. These were the last buses to enter service with full-width bonnet and exposed radiator, although on L51 the chrome has been given a coat of black paint. They also had a much-improved front destination display including a three-track number box. Withdrawal of the class began in 1964, although L51 would last until 1969. Standing just above the old alignment of the river, the tower and spire belong to the parish church of Our Lady and St Nicholas. Guns had once been positioned in the graveyard to ward off French invaders. Known to generations of seamen as the 'sailors' church', it was, with hundreds of other buildings, severely damaged during the heavy German air-raids which devastated much of Merseyside during 1940/1. Most of the attacks were aimed at destroying and disrupting the docks, but the 'collateral damage' extended to commercial and residential property. *Peter Roberts*

Left: Incorporating some parts from older cars, the 'Baby Grands' were in effect economy versions of the bogie 'Streamliners'. Intended mainly for use on street track, they outlived all other types, some 50 being still available for service in September 1957. Although not as smooth-riding as the bogie cars these four-wheelers, on their 9ft EMB flexible-axle trucks, still produced a good turn of speed, especially on the 'grass tracks'. Unfortunately their 60hp motors tended to overheat, while the bodywork, just like that on the bogie cars, was prone to water ingress. Trams ceased using the centre loop following conversion of the 29s on 3 April 1954, No 248 being seen on the final day of operation. To the right of the granite obelisk (erected after the loss of the *Titanic*) is the somewhat spartan frontage of the MDHB Riverside station (1895-1971), which was served by special boat trains direct to/from London via Edge Hill. Nearly two million troops passed through this station during World War 2. From the platforms passengers walked through the customs and immigration hall to embark onto the liners anchored at the stage. To the right, behind AEC Regent III A409 (HKF 885) on tram-replacement route 15, is the South-West building of Prince's Dock, since demolished for redevelopment. An extension to the Leeds & Liverpool Canal is currently planned, and this will allow narrow boats to pass almost exactly where car 248 is seen in this view. *J. B. C. McCann*

Right: From April 1954 to September 1957 only the south loop was still used by trams. In the first view, recorded on 5 March 1955, the last day of operation of the 10B, smoke rises from the 'Three Sisters' at Clarence Dock power station and from a single-stack 'Cunarder' anchored at the stage. To the left can be seen one of the covered bridges leading down to George's Landing Stage and the cross-river ferries. At high tide the floating stage and the connecting bridges would rise and fall, with all their parts groaning and creaking against the strain. Occasionally waves would break over the river wall, flooding the area to the left of the trams; even on reasonable days this open space could be bracing, and during the all-too-frequent bouts of inclement weather it felt very exposed, especially with so few places to shelter. Tram passengers had simply headed for the first car in line, but subsequently it became something of a guessing game, as the replacing buses were scattered all over the terminal area. Owing to the parlous state of its bodywork 'Liner' No 950 (10B) was nicknamed 'the mobile ruin'. In the second view, recorded on 16 May 1955, King Edward VII watches as a convoy of five 'Liners' encircle the loop. Fast and comfortable, the 163 high-capacity bogie cars were amongst the most stylish trams built in Britain during the 1930s. *J. B. C. McCann; Ray DeGroote*

The Corporation's batch of 50 all-Crossley DD42/7S buses, with their distinctive narrow radiators, became firm favourites with photographers. Dating from 1948/9, these 56-seaters were phased out between 1961 and 1964 and in their later years, being generally thirstier on fuel than other makes, were used mostly during peak hours. Seen on 5 July 1962 waiting to leave Mann Island on a short working of route 87B to Aigburth, C642 (JLV 127) carries an advertisement for the short-lived Hovercoach service linking the North Wirral coast and Rhyl; the world's first scheduled hovercraft service, this was operated intermittently during that summer by a Vickers-Armstrong VA-3 hovercraft owned by British United Airways. In the background, at the foot of James Street, is the imposing White Star Office Building (1896), designed by the same architect as the old Scotland Yard in London. It was here that White Star staff learned of the loss of the *Titanic*. Damaged by fire in 1923 and again during the bombing raids of World War 2, it would later be occupied by the Pacific Steam Navigation Co. *G. H. Pullin*

Right: The new bus station opened on 11 April 1965 occupied the northern end of George's Pier Head. It comprised 23 bays around the outside, plus an island with a further nine bays in which buses were parked herringbone-fashion. Access to the island was supposed to be via a subway, although most people risked crossing the road. Other facilities included shops, an information centre, an elevated promenade deck with views of the river and a first-floor restaurant. In this view are three of the rear-engined Leyland Atlanteans which came to dominate the Liverpool street scene. Trade-union opposition to higher-capacity vehicles had delayed their entry into regular service until 17 February 1963, but by 1967 there were 380 in service. In the 1960s significant numbers of people were still transferring from the buses to the ferries, but the days when more than 44% of Wallasey's adult working population was employed in Liverpool were long gone. The loss of jobs, the advent of evening television, the growth in car ownership and the run-down of the ferries made the bus station redundant. Furthermore, too much of the poorly constructed building had suffered from the effects of the wind-blown salt spray. It was initially closed to accommodate a John Lennon Memorial Concert which took place on 5 May 1990 and, after a brief reopening, finally closed in 1991. *Mike Mercer*

Right: The area to the south of the Dock Board building is known as Mann Island. This became the point of departure for all Crosville services, including long-distance express routes like the X61 (introduced in November 1963), the number referring to the M6 and M1 motorways which had recently been joined to provide a north–south link. Even so, the journey time from Liverpool to Victoria Coach Station was still seven hours. CRL262 (TFM 262K), a Leyland-engined ECW-bodied Bristol RE of 1972, was one of the last Crosville coaches to be delivered in this attractive cream-and-black livery. The column to the left behind the vehicles is the Merchant Navy Memorial, dedicated to those merchant seamen who lost their lives during World War 2. The brick building on the far left was a rest home for elderly people and has since been demolished. Mann Island still serves as a bus terminus in 2007. *Peter Jackson*

This highly evocative streetscape recorded in May 1955 features so much that has disappeared. Known locally as the 'Dockers' Umbrella', the Liverpool Overhead Railway (1893-1956) had been the world's first electrically powered elevated railway. Here a northbound train rumbles into Pier Head, the busiest and most substantial station on the line, while underneath is Jesse Hartley's 'Line of Docks Railway'. To the right are the Goree Piazzas (1793-1958) — arcaded warehouses long associated with the infamous triangular trade whereby a quarter of all Liverpool ships were involved in transporting slaves. Even after the last 'blackbirder' sailed from the port in 1807, much of the city's wealth still depended on the slave-worked cotton plantations in the southern United States. Underneath the Threlfall's sign at the north end of the block is Tom Hall's pub, Threlfall's being one of the city's oldest breweries. Another once familiar sight were the steam 'waggons'. Heading into The Strand is a six-ton Sentinel of 1924; subsequently converted into a tractor, from 1950 to 1960 it belonged to Edward Billington (Criddles) Ltd and is now preserved. In the foreground is one of the city's distinctive enamel tram stops; red signified compulsory, and blue request. Note also the Standard Vanguard car, registered to the military. *Ray DeGroote*

Ray DeGroote was an American enthusiast who visited the city for a few days in May 1955. He took a series of unique colour images on slide film. Some of the colour has faded over the years, but the majority has been recovered digitally. In the first picture 'Liner' No 916, having ascended Water Street, passes the Town Hall at 11.51am on 18 May. Situated in the heart of the business district, this is the second-oldest building of note in the central area. Dating from 1754 but reconstructed to designs by James Wyatt following a fire in 1795, it contains several magnificent rooms as well as many works of art. Following removal of the trams from Castle Street, a striking new red road surface provided an impressive approach, and many local celebrities have acknowledged excited crowds from the Town Hall balcony. The white stone building (1926) behind was the head office of Martins Bank (now part of Barclays), one of the city's oldest and most influential banks. In 1940 Britain's gold reserves were housed in its vaults *en route* to Canada. On the opposite corner the old head office of Martins was now occupied by the District Bank. Liverpool has always been a city of contrasts, and bowler-hatted city gents from 'over the water' or the more affluent suburbs served by the electric trains to Ormskirk and Southport could still be seen in the 1960s. In the second picture, taken on the same day, No 182 of 1937 is outbound along Dale Street to Lower Lane via Breck Road. During the 19th century this ancient thoroughfare was straightened, creating a canyon flanked on either side by solid Victorian civic and commercial buildings. Something of the area's earlier history survives in the names of nearby 'jiggers' (alleyways) such as Hackins Hey (to the right of the tram), Quaker's Alley and Leather Lane. Trams last ran along Dale Street on 3 November 1956. Many short-stage passengers would be lost from May 1966, when both Dale Street and Water Street became one-way in the river direction. *Ray DeGroote*

Left: Nearly all the coaching inns in Dale Street were swept away during the mid-Victorian building boom, although 'The Angel' survived until 1962. Here one of the early Atlanteans, L531 (531 KD), bound for the Pier Head on 8 June 1969, has passed the Municipal Buildings (1866) complete with clock tower, the terracotta Liverpool, London & Globe head office (1886), the Temple (1864) and the begrimed Royal Insurance building (1903) on the corner of North John Street. The destination blinds have already been set for the return journey to Kirkby on route 44D. People living in the suburbs usually had a choice of routes, some using Dale Street and others Church Street; in bus days the 'D' suffix meant 'via Dale Street', as opposed to 'C' via Church Street. It was the custom for conductors to change the blinds as the bus progressed through the central area to allow for a smoke and a quick 'cuppa' at Pier Head. *Cedric Greenwood*

Right: Besides the trams, buses and cars, many streets in the central area were filled with a rich mix of commercial vehicles, including a fascinating array of lorries. Seen at the tunnel end of Dale Street, a well-laden Leyland eight-wheeler of 1955 heads towards the Docks. Owned by W. H. Bowker of Blackburn, it is probably carrying fruit, at the time the company's main business. In the background is the former Central Technical College. The photograph was taken on 23 May 1966, just after Dale Street became one-way; the lorry is seen close to the site of the present-day exit ramp of the Churchill Way South flyover. Although the flyovers alleviated congestion in the central area they also led to fewer people using the buses. By the early 1980s hardly anyone was going to the Pier Head, and this once-thriving business district gradually fell into the doldrums, with the loss of some 30,000 office-based jobs. Former commercial offices have now been transformed for residential use, including the premises on the extreme right of the picture, which early in 2007 were being converted into flats. *Peter J. Davies*

Left: On leaving Derby Square trams served the Church Street area, the commercial heart of the city, with its shops, restaurants, hotels, cinemas and theatres. Here bogie car No 766 pauses outside the Midland Bank (now the Trials Hotel) in July 1953. Built at Edge Lane Works in 1931, it was one of 12 air-braked cars on English Electric trucks, these 70-seat vehicles helping to transform the image of the Liverpool fleet by offering a higher degree of speed and comfort. All but three were modernised and re-trucked between 1937 and 1944. Housed at Edge Lane depot, the last five were withdrawn in March 1955; No 766 was a firm favourite with enthusiasts and was hired for two tours of the system. In 1977 No 762, which for 20 years had served as a bowling shelter at Newsham Park, was rescued for restoration by the Merseyside Tramway Preservation Society and, resplendent in its original 1931 livery of red and cream, now operates on the Wirral Heritage Tramway. *J. B. C. McCann*

Above: A rare 1938 view of South Castle Street. This had been the starting point for the first electric tram route (November 1898) and latterly served as the second major tram terminus, routes terminating here officially showing red-on-white (as opposed to white-on-black) numbers until 1947. In the centre of the picture is the enquiry office, where free timetables were available. Car 17, in the old red livery, was one of many four-wheel, open-fronted Priestly 'Standards' built by the Corporation during the 1920s; after the war most unmodernised 'Standards' would be fitted with crude wood-and-canvas drivers' windscreens. The domed Queen Victoria Memorial stands on the site of Liverpool Castle, the last remnants of which were knocked down early in the 18th century to make way for St George's Church (1734-1900). The tower in the background (left) carries advertisements for the *Daily Dispatch* and *Daily Sketch*, two long-defunct national newspapers, while in front of it is Preeson's Row, which would be wiped out during the Blitz; both the Victoria Memorial and the National Bank (the large white stone building) would survive. *G. D. Parry collection*

Left: Although trams ceased using South Castle Street in September 1951 a track around the Victoria Memorial was retained for emergencies. In one of those interesting transport quirks a single scheduled hospital journey used this loop every Sunday morning for another six years. Even after the trams had gone the fossilised rails remained embedded in the setts. *En route* to its terminus in South John Street in June 1964 is a Northern Counties-bodied Guy Arab IV, one of the last batch delivered to Lancashire United Transport (LUT). Behind the British Railways Morris delivery van, on the north side of St George's Crescent, is the Pearl Assurance building; this had replaced an Austen Reed store destroyed in the bombing between August 1940 and May 1941, when more than 2,700 people were killed, 120,000 houses destroyed or damaged, and schools, hospitals and churches obliterated, tram services on several occasions being confined to the fringes of the central area as a result. *J. N. Barlow / Online Transport Archive*

Above: From 1951 to 1974 South John Street was the starting-point for inter-urban services 39, 317 and 320. Duties on the 317 (St Helens via Prescot) were covered by Ribble and St Helens Corporation, whilst those on the 320 (Wigan via St Helens and Haydock) were shared additionally with LUT and Wigan Corporation. In this view are two Leyland PD2s of differing appearance. Wigan No 34 (FEK 7F) of 1968 combines a traditional exposed radiator with a forward-entrance Massey body, whereas St Helens 178 (LDJ 988) of 1960 has a concealed radiator but a traditional open-platform body by East Lancs. Seen hugging the kerb underneath the St Helens bus is the paved wagonway installed to prevent slipping when loaded horse-drawn wagons tackled steep gradients. Overlooking the 1960s buildings in the foreground are the turrets of the much-loved Liverpool Sailors' Home (1847-1973), the interior of which featured decks reminiscent of sailing ships, while to the right is Canning Place, site of the first dock (1715) and later the Custom House, bombed in 1941. This whole area has since been taken over by today's Liverpool One complex. *Peter Jackson*

Below: Dating from 1956, A166 (SKB 166) was one of a batch of AEC Regent Vs with bodywork built at Edge Lane on Crossley frames. Wearing the predominantly green livery (with cream window surrounds) introduced in 1960, it is pictured turning out of Whitechapel to join other buses at the loading points in Sir Thomas Street, in the company of Ford Zephyrs and a Consul, an Austin A40 and one of the once-ubiquitous Austin FX3 taxicabs. Such a manœuvre cannot be executed today: in May 1966 the traffic flow here would be reversed as part of a major one-way scheme, and today Whitechapel is pedestrianised at this point. Heading towards Dale Street, the GPO van has probably just left the Head Post Office (1899), which important building — another victim of the 1941 air-raids — had been partially rebuilt. At one time some sections remained open 24 hours a day, with a night-mail service, Monday to Fridays only, until 9pm. Fortunately some of the building has been retained and incorporated into the Metquarter shopping centre. *G. D. Parry*

Right: For more than 140 years Church Street has been Liverpool's principal shopping thoroughfare. In its heyday people poured in from places as far afield as the Potteries and North Wales, and long queues formed at the various bus and tram stops, especially on Saturdays. The many stores included Bunney's, Cooper's, Henderson's, George Henry Lee's, C&A, Burton's, Woolworth's (the first branch in the UK), Wynn's and Littlewood's. The Tatler news cinema screened continuous programmes of cartoons, pictorials and newsreels lasting an hour and 20 minutes, while the upper windows of the Kardomah café provided a superb vantage-point for watching the lines of trams and buses whilst eating delicious potato croquettes. This view was recorded the day before Church Street was pedestrianised; from 16 March 1974 the busiest and most lucrative loading-points in the city would no longer exist. Seen on City Circle route 100 in the green livery applied 1971-3 is 1051 (FKF 930F), one of 110 OMO MCW-bodied Leyland Panthers delivered during 1968/9. The Swiss-registered Opel seems to have come a long way on 'L' plates. *K. W. Swallow*

Left: An action-packed view at the bottom of Ranelagh Street — a location known officially as Waterloo Place but more often as Boots Corner (left). In the foreground is one of a dwindling number of telegraph boys; years earlier many young men had been employed conveying messages between offices. The date is September 1957, and the end of tramway operation is just a few days away. Still looking reasonably smart, 'Baby Grand' No 224 makes for the Pier Head by way of Church Street; during rush hours some trams short-worked to Clayton Square. To the right is AEC Regent III A759 (MKB 952), one of the first batch of 50 8ft-wide vehicles with 56-seat Crossley bodywork delivered in 1951/2, the majority of which would survive until 1968. Their extra width allowed for the introduction of a more comprehensive destination display. Route 76 served future Prime Minister Harold Wilson's Huyton constituency. *J. B. C. McCann*

Above: In this very rare colour view from 1938 a solicitous cabbie eyes a group of well-heeled ladies emerging from Central station. Two Priestly 'Standards', one in the post-1933 green-and-white livery, make slow progress uphill towards Ranelagh Place and the busy junction with Lime Street. In 1931 the track on Ranelagh Street had been doubled as part of an early traffic-management scheme aimed at relieving congestion in this central shopping area. Most buildings at the top end of the street would be destroyed in the Blitz of May 1941; these included the prestigious David Lewis department store (Lewis's) and Jacob's, the tailors, with its distinctive tower (background, right). Horse-drawn traffic, especially around the docks, would be still in evidence 25 years later. *G. D. Parry collection*

Although it is no longer possible to turn from Ranelagh Street into Church Street the majority of buildings remain today, including (in the background) the postwar Lewis's and the Adelphi Hotel. Arriving on route H5 from Warrington on 4 August 1970 is forward-entrance Bristol Lodekka DFG258 (SFM 258F), with 70-seat body by Eastern Coach Works. Dating from 1967, this was one of the final batch of half-cab vehicles delivered to Crosville. On the extreme right is the frontage of Liverpool Central station, opened in 1874. Built by the Cheshire Lines Committee, it was reached by a series of tunnels and a steep sandstone cutting. Closed in 1972, it was replaced by an unprepossessing shopping centre; Central Low Level, opened in 1892 by the Mersey Railway, survives as part of the current Merseyrail network. Off to the right is upmarket Bold Street, home in the 1930s to stores such as Waring & Gillow and Jaeger. *K. W. Swallow*

At Owen Owen (right) in Parker Street the customer was 'always right'. Founded by the son of a Welsh farmer, it prided itself on good customer and labour relations. This prestigious store was built on what had been the north side of Clayton Square. Outside, especially on Saturdays, large queues formed at the many staggered bus stops. Both vehicles pictured belonged to the first batch of 200 Mk II Atlanteans delivered 1962-4, the Metro-Cammell bodywork having been built to Liverpool specifications. Unlike L699 (699 KD), L650 (650 KD) on the right has been converted for one-man operation, the reduced destination display giving the game away. However, moves towards OMO had met with strong union opposition, so in 1970, when the photograph was taken, L699 would have been carrying a conductor. The buildings in the background include Littlewoods' Spinney House, completed in the mid-1950s. Parker Street and Elliot Street had been one-way since 1960, but in 1986 the whole area would be pedestrianised, and Clayton Square, including some 200-year-old buildings, demolished as part of a shopping redevelopment. In 1994 the Owen Owen building was put to different retail use, including a Tesco Metro on the ground floor. *Mike Mercer*

Left: As early as 1947 the Corporation had operated some limited-stop buses on routes serving the more far-flung suburbs. Starting in May 1954, a small network of limited-stop 5xx-series services was built up along some of the busiest corridors. By July 1955 the first of these, the 500, was taking 67 minutes from Kirkby to Speke via Lime Street, with extra buses starting from the city. Crossley C631 (JLV 116) was photographed outside Lime Street station shortly before withdrawal in 1963. In November 1969 the 500 would be the first double-deck route to become one-man-operated. All the buildings behind, including the Punch & Judy café and the Royal Hotel, would be replaced in the late 1960s by yet more anonymous buildings. Gloucester Street, the short approach road to the south of the once-opulent railway-owned North Western Hotel (1871), was used for vehicle access to Lime Street station. Located at the end of a long, steep cutting (originally cable-worked), the first station on this site dated from 1836; today's building, with its splendid pair of elliptical roofs, dates mostly from the period 1867-71. *J. M. Ryan*

Left: Lime Street in June 1964, with not a private car in sight. By far the widest thoroughfare in the city, it proved ideal for parades and demonstrations. Incredibly, whilst St George's Hall (right) was undergoing renovation, the sweep of majestic Victorian buildings in the background, which had housed the Territorial Army HQ, the Caledonia Pub and the one-time Grand, Imperial and Washington hotels, was in the course of demolition to make way for St John's Precinct. Many older Liverpudlians will remember standing to watch the landmark Guinness Clock and the illuminated moving news screen at night. The open space in front of the old hotels, known as The Quadrant, had once served as another tram terminus. Pursued by a GPO Morris van, Leyland PD2 L361 (WKF 217) pulls towards the kerb to offload passengers, probably heading for the station. *J. N. Barlow / Online Transport Archive*

From the mid-1930s to the late 1960s the Corporation purchased relatively few single-deckers. Amongst them were four underfloor-engined Leyland Royal Tigers — SL171-4 (SKB 168-71) — with dual-door Crossley bodies assembled at Edge Lane. Acquired to experiment with one-man operation in 1956, they aroused considerable opposition from the trade unions. Eventually all four were comprehensively rebuilt by Metro-Cammell as 1½-deck coaches for use on an express service to the Airport, the design having been modelled on an American Greyhound vehicle seen by the General Manager in a trade magazine, the space under the raised section being used for luggage. Painted in two shades of blue, they were renumbered XL171-4. After a new airport service worked by specially adapted Atlanteans was introduced in 1966 the single-deckers were transferred to the summer-only service taking passengers from Lime Street station to the Irish and Isle of Man ferries. No XL174 (SKB 171) is seen at the bottom of Skelhorne Street on 24 May 1970, when both St John's Precinct and St George's Hotel were under construction. Having passed to the PTE, all four were sold during 1973/4, and one is now preserved. *Alan Murray-Rust*

Left: For many years Lime Street (formerly Limekiln Lane) enjoyed something of an unsavoury reputation with 'Maggie Mays' walking the street. Over the years this famous thoroughfare has witnessed sectarian conflicts and riots, police and transport strikes as well as victory parades and enthusiastic welcomes for national and international stars. It was also immortalised by local writer Alun Owen in his play *No Trams to Lime Street*, which turned out to be a prophetic title. When this picture was taken on 30 July 1955 'Liner' No 956 was outbound on the eight-mile, hour-long journey to Kirkby. Just over two years later Liverpudlians would assemble on the steps outside St George's Hall to watch the final procession of 13 cars, after which there really were no trams to Lime Street — or anywhere else. *D. G. Clarke*

Above: In the 1950s most buildings were caked in layers of industrial grime and soot produced by the thousands of belching chimneys which also contributed to the city's notorious 'pea-souper' fogs, when an eerie silence fell on the streets, and other road users gratefully followed the trams on their fixed tracks. Inbound on route 13 from Lower Lane in 1954, 'Liner' No 889 of 1936 coasts down William Brown Street past the Walker Art Gallery (1877), Picton Reading Room (1879) and Free Library (1860). Its driver will no doubt take extra care on the steep descent to the junction with Byrom Street; in January 1945 an out-of-control sister car had careered down London Road, striking another tram broadside-on as it turned from Dale Street into Byrom Street, both vehicles toppling over, with fatal consequences. Behind, approaching one of the art-deco 1930s street lamps erected in the area around the Queensway road tunnel, is one of a series of 90 Daimler CV double-deckers new in 1949, while in the far distance a cherry-red Ribble bus passes Rushworth & Dreaper, the music store in Islington. To the right is Commutation Row, with its mix of shops including a Burton's, a jeweller's and two pubs — the Court House and the Hare & Hounds; this site is now occupied by a modern office block. Today William Brown Street has no through traffic. *J. B. C. McCann*

Left: Liverpool has boasted many fine buildings, some tragically lost during the Blitz, others demolished during the planning purges initiated in the 1960s. At one point it was even feared St George's Hall might go the same way. Designed by Henry Lonsdale Elmes and opened in 1854, this is one of Europe's outstanding neo-classical buildings. Between the Hall and Old Haymarket are St John's Gardens (1904), laid out on the site of a former church and cemetery. The gardens and the perimeter of the Hall are adorned with statues of (among others) Robert Peel, William Gladstone, Father Nugent, George Stephenson and William Rathbone; there is also a plaque to French prisoners who died in Liverpool during the Napoleonic wars. The Corporation and Ribble half-cab double-deckers are dwarfed by the 60ft black granite column which once adorned the tunnel entrance. The art-deco style of the 1930s was reflected in the attractive green toll booths and tall lamp standards which illuminated the tunnel portal. Later, in a move aimed at relieving congestion, all traffic movements across the tunnel mouth were banned. *G. H. Hesketh*

Above In connection with the opening of the tunnel the track layout at Old Haymarket was remodelled in 1933. Subsequently, in 1950, the through tracks were abandoned, leaving a three-track, peak-hour terminus which survived until 1956. Other 'workers' rush-hour queue points' (as they were officially described by the Corporation) for trams existed in the mid-1950s at Roe Street, Commutation Row, North John Street and Great Crosshall Street. Here 'Liner' 914 waits by the red enamel stop, queuing-point for cars on the 6/6A; the other, maroon sign directed people towards Exchange station. In the background can be seen the Co-op's Unity House, where, it was said, the legendary MP for Liverpool Exchange, Bessie Braddock, 'always bought her hats'; the large billboard advertises 'International Co-operation Day Celebration'. On the opposite corner stands the ornate City Technical College (1901). All buildings on Byrom Street were demolished when the road was widened in an attempt to solve the congestion caused by vehicles queuing to enter the tunnel, especially during evening peak hours. Old Haymarket would survive as a bus terminus until 1986. *J. B. C. McCann*

In 1956 the loss-making Woodside night ferry was replaced by a jointly operated Birkenhead–Liverpool bus service through the Queensway Tunnel, each municipality providing a single bus on a three-monthly rotation. Liverpool used a pair of recently delivered, single-door Crossley-bodied underfloor-engined Leyland Royal Tigers. Always kept in good condition, SL175/6 (SKB 172/3) were also used for private-hire work and carried permanent 'PRIVATE' destination displays. At first fares were paid to the tunnel's toll-collector, but when all toll collection was transferred to the Wirral side they were collected by the bus driver. Behind SL176 on 25 October 1965 can be seen the entrance to the four-lane tunnel, built at the end of the Depression; central government provided some of the money (£7 million) to relieve chronic unemployment in a city where more than a quarter of men were out of work. Both Liverpool vehicles eventually passed to the PTE; after serving for a time as ordinary buses they were withdrawn in 1972, although SL175 was retained until June 1975 as a Traveller Ticket sales bus. *Brian Faragher*

Illustrating some of the changes introduced upon the opening in 1971 of a second under-river tunnel, a trio of buses stand outside Exchange station in Tithebarn Street in June 1974. Absorbing an orderly queue, Crosville dual-purpose ECW-bodied Bristol RELL ERG278 (YFM 278L) is on route 418, which, together with the 419, provided the first under-river 'Rapidride' services; behind, with a less orderly queue, is a PTE Alexander-bodied Atlantean on the 92B to Kirkby, while in the background can be seen a Wirral Division Atlantean on one of the 'Cross River Express' routes serving Wallasey. Such services further eroded traffic on the two remaining ferries and also put pressure on the Merseyrail electric services. When the rail services from Southport and Ormskirk were re-routed in May 1977 onto the underground Link line a new station was opened at nearby Moorfields. Exchange station was closed, but the impressive 1888 frontage was retained, cleaned and incorporated into a new retail/office complex. *A. F. Gahan*

Some street scenes in the northern suburbs have undergone radical alterations during the past 50 years. For example, construction of the approach roads to the second under-river road tunnel cut a swathe through the tightly packed terraced housing centred on Scotland Road, laid out in 1803. Also set to disappear were the 1930s-style Corporation flats on the left. The opening of the Wallasey tunnel (officially the Kingsway Tunnel) on 28 June 1971 led to the introduction of all-day 'Cross River Express' routes linking Liverpool and Wallasey. These services were operated by the Merseyside Passenger Transport Executive, which had been created by the merger in December 1969 of the passenger-transport departments of Liverpool, Birkenhead and Wallasey Corporations. Painted in the PTE's recently introduced Wirral Division livery (an amalgam of Birkenhead blue and Wallasey cream), the bus has just left the tunnel and is heading for the city centre on the first day of the service. It was one of a batch of 13 dual-door Northern Counties-bodied Atlanteans ordered by Birkenhead but not delivered until after the PTE takeover, in 1970/1. In hot pursuit is a typical 'wagon and drag' lorry plus a profusion of locally built Ford Anglia cars. *J. M. Ryan*

Right: It is the early 1960s, and D516 (JKC 141), a 56-seat Northern Counties-bodied Daimler CVA6 of 1949, is heading towards the industrial part of Vauxhall Road. Numerically, this was the first of a batch of 90 Daimler CVs delivered in 1949/50 as part of the tram-replacement programme. Those with Daimler engines were classified CVD6, those with AEC CVA6, all having pre-selective gearboxes. Associated for many years with the north of the city, they had bodywork by Northern Counties (50) and Weymann (40) finished at Edge Lane. Route 16 had been converted to bus operation in December 1950, but in Vauxhall Road, as in many former tram streets, the traction poles were retained to support street lighting. Few Liverpool buses were sold for further service, most going straight to scrap merchants; very few of the Daimlers, phased out between 1960 and 1966, carried any more passengers, D516 being despatched to a dealer in Lanark in 1964.
H. B. Christiansen

Right: When it closed in December 1956 the Overhead Railway was replaced by Corporation routes 1-1E, although subsequently the poor condition of sections of the Dock Road would lead to diversions and re-routeings. Dwindling passenger loadings led to the introduction in June 1969 of OMO single-deckers. Pictured heading south is 2010 (SKB 680G), one of a batch of 25 rear-engined Bristol REs with 45-seat Park Royal bodywork, these being the last new buses to enter service with the Corporation. It has just crossed the bascule bridge (still in place today) connecting Collingwood and Stanley Docks, the latter being the only dock on the inland side of the Dock Road; in 1848 a flight of locks had provided a much-needed link between the Leeds & Liverpool Canal and the River Mersey. Towering over the scene is the colossal Stanley New Warehouse (1900). Built with blue and red bricks, this was one of the largest bonded warehouses in the world, capable of housing a staggering 65,000,000lb of tobacco. Although its long-term future remains uncertain the 'tobacco warehouse' stands as a reminder of Liverpool's long-standing trading associations with the USA, notably in the importation of cotton and timber, as well as tobacco. *J. M. Ryan*

Left: Over the years almost every kind of cargo has been handled by the Mersey Docks & Harbour Board (MDHB). Here, in 1969, hundreds watch the world-famous LNER Pacific *Flying Scotsman* being winched on to the freighter *Saxonia* by the Dock Board crane *Mammoth*; four years later, somewhat the worse for wear after a fraught stay in the USA, No 4472 would return home, again through the Port of Liverpool. In May 1958 Liverpool's last tram, 'Baby Grand' No 293, also set sail for the New World. Sixty years before that some of the city's first electric trams had come the other way; built at the J. G. Brill factory in Philadelphia, these were a group of centre-entrance, single-deck bogie cars, three of which were later rebuilt as 100-seat open-toppers with the nautical nickname 'Oceanics' after the White Star liner of the time. *J. G. Parkinson / Online Transport Archive*

Below left: By the late 1960s horse-drawn traffic had all but disappeared, so it was certainly worth photographing one of the last slow-moving carts to plod along the overcrowded Dock Road. Much has been written about the sectarian divide in and around the Dock Estate; suffice it to say that before World War 1 nearly all 11,000 carters would have come from the Protestant community, whilst the majority of unskilled labour would have been Catholic. Increasing mechanisation and containerisation has seen the workforce plummet, although significantly more tonnage is handled. Behind the parked cars is the MDHB double-track railway, the dock wall and *Mammoth*. This floating crane had a fascinating history, having been built for the Tsarist government in Russia. The sale fell through after the Russian Revolution and it was sold instead to the MDHB, arriving in November 1920. Despite being damaged several times during World War 2 (and reputedly repaired at the insistence of Winston Churchill because of its importance to the war effort) it served on the Mersey until 1986. Owned by a Swedish company and renamed *Baltic Mammoth*, it is still at work in Scandinavian waters. *J. G. Parkinson / Online Transport Archive*

Right and below right: The one-time transport hub at Seaforth has altered beyond all recognition, this area now being enclosed within the secure area of the current Dock Estate. Framed by the cranes of Gladstone Dock, generations of Corporation trams and buses terminated in Regent Road in the then Borough of Bootle. To cater for thousands of dock estate workers regular routes were supplemented at peak times by a network of industrial services, and it was from here in February 1951 that Bootle's last tram left on a 'dockers' special'. As the workforce declined and car ownership increased, the need for such services almost disappeared. The two buses in the first photograph enjoyed long lives: L252 (VKB 708), a 1956 Leyland PD2/20 with Crossley bodywork, remained with the PTE, cut down as a towing vehicle, until the 1980s, while A267 (VKB 900), a 1957 AEC Regent V with Metro-Cammell Orion body, survives in preservation. The viaduct seen in both views carried the Lancashire & Yorkshire Railway's North Mersey branch (1866), most of which would later be electrified with the third-rail system. On the north side of Rimrose Bridge (bottom view) was the site of the one-time LOR Seaforth Sands station and carriage sheds. From 1900 to 1925 a feeder tram service ran from here to Waterloo and Great Crosby. The bus emerging from under the bridge, in October 1970, is Ribble 1771 (RCK 916), one of more than 100 Metro-Cammell-bodied Leyland PD3/5s delivered 1961-3. Today the bridge has gone, the road is the major dual carriageway taking traffic north towards Waterloo and Crosby, and the area in the distance (left) has been redeveloped as the Royal Seaforth Dock.
Roy Marshall / Photobus; A. F. Gahan

Left: As it weaves its way out of the city to the north the Leeds & Liverpool Canal is crossed by many bridges, but only one of these, at Litherland, was a lift bridge. The barriers would come down, and the central section of the bridge would rise, giving sufficient air draught for the barge to pass underneath but leading to delays for road users. This, coupled with predicted increases in traffic following the construction of Seaforth container terminal, made it necessary to build a new dual carriageway by-passing the old bridge; this structure was then taken out completely, leaving Bridge Road without a bridge. Crossing on 14 November 1971, shortly before the bridge was demolished, is Ribble 1604 (KCK 850), one of a batch of 105 Burlingham-bodied 72-seat Leyland PD3/4s delivered in 1957/8. Sporting full-width cabs, these were Ribble's first 30ft-long double-deckers and proved ideal for the heavily patronised routes into central Liverpool.
A. F. Gahan

Left: Of all the former tram depots converted into bus garages Litherland was the smallest. Located in Linacre Road, it had been extended and given a modern façade in 1939, the last trams leaving in 1950. The four sections were lettered A-D, the last being on the site of the former horse tram shed. Contrasting with the situation at some other garages, vehicle movements at Litherland were an integral part of the local street scene. On 17 February 1973 an AEC Regent V stands outside Section A, a Leyland PD2 peers out from Section B, whilst three Bristol REs huddle in Section C, their reversed cream-and-green livery denoting their OMO capability. After its closure in October 1986 the garage remained in use for a short time as a vehicle store. The site is now occupied by a Somerfield supermarket. *Alan Atkinson*

As the principal artery linking Liverpool with Bootle and the suburbs of Waterloo and Crosby, Stanley Road carried very heavy bus and tram traffic, and in the final days of the trams (1950) the track along this street was in appalling condition. The Ribble routes included the 50 series, operated jointly with the Corporation. Half-cab 1481 (JRN 48) was one of a batch of 25 61-seat Metro-Cammell-bodied Leyland PD2/12s dating from 1956. Unlike some other Ribble double-deckers of the period they had no platform doors. The Cambrian Airways advertisement enticed potential travellers to 'Come fly with me'. This part of Stanley Road remains much the same today. When this view was recorded on 23 August 1970 some of the shops, including a small Tesco's, were still trading; others were empty, some boarded up. *A. F. Gahan*

Left: During the war parts of Bootle had been severely damaged. In the 1960s a major regeneration scheme centred on the New Strand complex, which included houses, shops and offices, some accommodating relocated government departments. The scene here is overlooked by the completed Strand Tower and the Triad building under construction. In August 1968 long-established orbital routes 60, 81 and 81D were diverted to serve a new bus station. On leaving they travelled along Washington Parade, a new highway constructed following removal of a low canal bridge. The inter-suburban 81D reached Speke (Eastern Avenue) by way of Queens Drive and Woolton. No A221 (VKB 819) belonged to a batch of 30 AEC Regent Vs with 62-seat MCW-framed bodies completed at Edge Lane which, owing to a slow-down in demand for public transport, entered service between September 1957 and October 1959. This example was one of 18 unpainted vehicles in the fleet. An experiment to see if it reduced maintenance costs, the practice was never widely implemented. The test vehicles, however, remained unpainted until withdrawal by the PTE, some of them looking decidedly shabby in their latter days. *A. F. Gahan*

Left: By the late 1950s the Corporation was looking to invest in high-capacity double-deckers. To this end three experimental vehicles (E1-3) were fully assessed, the first to enter service being E3 (116 TMD) in January 1959. This was a lowbridge, chassisless AEC Bridgemaster with 30ft Park Royal body and seats for 76 — 14 more than on the more conventional buses of the period. No E3 was the last AEC purchased by the Corporation. Here it stands in Carisbrooke Road, Walton, terminus of several routes including the cross-city former tram 25 to Aigburth. Off camera (left) was Walton garage, which finally closed its doors in 1989 and was demolished in 1998. Withdrawn in 1973, E3 survives in preservation. *Roy Marshall / Photobus*

Forming part of the main A59 to Preston and the north, Scotland Road and Kirkdale Road were served by both Corporation and Ribble buses. Seen in October 1973, inbound for Skelhorne Street bus station on route 101 from Preston via Ormskirk and Maghull, is Ribble 1553 (KCK 914), one of a batch of Burlingham-bodied Leyland PD3/4s delivered in 1957/8. The bus has been newly repainted in the poppy-red livery adopted by the National Bus Company in 1972, but the Metro-Cammell-bodied PD3/5 behind retains the more traditional Ribble red. During the past half-century this thoroughfare, together with many neighbouring streets, has changed almost beyond recognition. As tightly knit communities with their own local shops and small businesses were dispersed, often only churches and pubs remained. In the background, beyond the recently delivered PTE Leyland Atlantean, is the 'Goat's Head', with its distinctive ornamentation, on the corner of Smith Street (now landscaped); this was one of many pubs owned by Higson's, then the city's oldest brewery (1780). As part of the evolution of the Liverpool street scene the buildings on the left, which replaced Victorian three-storey blocks after the war, have themselves now been demolished. Route 101, meanwhile, disappeared without replacement in March 1975, but 1553, withdrawn along with the rest of its batch in the early 1970s, survives in preservation. *A. F. Gahan*

The mass demolition of the 1960s and '70s rendered some areas of the city virtually unrecognisable. In this May 1970 view L170 (RKC 271), one of 30 Alexander-bodied Leyland PD2/20s delivered in 1954/5, descends Eastbourne Street, which would close to all traffic in August 1972 and has long since vanished. To the far left had been the ancient township of Everton, once a leafy village. During the 19th-century building boom this steep slope between Everton Road and Shaw Street was occupied by elegant three-storey houses complete with substantial frontages and wrought-iron balconies, as well as more-affordable dwellings. Most were constructed by Welsh builders, who, bringing with them their own language, settled in several parts of the city. Owing to the narrowness of the roads and the severity of the gradients, outbound and inbound tram tracks were laid in different streets. This site is now occupied by Everton Park. *A. F. Gahan*

Once-bustling Everton Road is still recognisable today, albeit much altered. When photographed on 7 September 1970, 1135 (UKA 586H) was barely six months old. It was one of the first batch of Atlanteans known, on account of their increased length (33ft), as 'Jumbos'. Although ordered by the Corporation these dual-door Alexander-bodied 79-seaters entered service after the PTE takeover. Tram-replacement route 33 (Everton Road–Seaforth) would finally disappear in 1986. *A. F. Gahan*

Left: Few colour views exist of trams on the streets in some inner sections of town. The narrow parts of Breck Road/Townsend Lane had both single and interlaced track, movements being controlled by coloured light signals. This picture features a car leaving the 200yd length of single track in Townsend Lane in May 1955. The Breck Road routes (13/14) would be withdrawn six months later, although by then 'Liner' No 175 of 1937 would already be withdrawn. The cream-and-red Austin K-series lorry parked in Bishop Street was owned by Reece & Sons, a well-known local dairy and confectioner's, and may have been delivering to the two adjacent grocers, Fields and Lees. Partially obscured by the advertising hoarding is the Elm House pub at the corner of Lampeter Road, which is still serving today. *Ray DeGroote*

Left: Liverpool had several railways encircling the suburbs, and railway bridges, like this one at Clubmoor, sometimes caused breaks in the 'grass track', the trams reverting to short lengths of street running. The run-down of trams on Utting Avenue (left) was completed in 1951. The red enamel stop sign on the traction pole was one of the oldest still *in situ* in 1955. The oil between the rails showed where the stops were situated, and the bollards, positioned at the entrance to each length of 'grass track', warned other road users not to trespass on the reservations. Beyond the girder bridge the well-designed suburbs were served by long stretches of 'grass track', the 14s peeling away along Utting Avenue East, whilst the 13s continued straight ahead to join the routes along East Lancashire Road. Following conversion of the 13 and 14, on Bonfire Night 1955, 35 'Streamliners' went for scrap. The railway bridge carried the North Liverpool loop line (Cheshire Lines Committee, 1879), which had seen heavy wartime traffic. Despite the opening of new stations in the 1920s the line would close to passengers in 1960, Grand National specials in 1963 and goods traffic in 1979. The trackbed is now used as a footpath-cum-cycleway. *Ray DeGroote*

Between the wars the Corporation built a range of quality housing in the north-eastern suburbs. Integral to the plan was a first-rate public transport system, consisting of many miles of segregated tramway reservation. The elegant poles supported both the street lighting and the neat, unobtrusive overhead wires which had been erected for use by bow-collectors, even though Liverpool retained traditional trolley poles to the end. The two-mile central reservation along Walton Hall Avenue and East Lancashire Road, as far as Lower Lane, was completed by 1938. Several labour-intensive factories also provided a source of local employment. As a result, in peak hours many additional cars were operated from Walton depot, the 78-seat bogie cars proving particularly effective crowd-swallowers. On 30 July 1955, flanked by some rather overgrown privet hedges, 'Liner' No 889 was photographed outbound towards Lower Lane. Routes 19/44 were replaced on 3 November 1956 at the start of the Suez oil crisis. The next day 889 and 30 sister cars made a final one-way trip along these tracks to the depths of the Kirkby Trading Estate. Here they meet a fiery end despite growing demands by press and public for trams to be restored to routes 19/44. *D. G. Clarke*

Left and below left: The major tramway hub in Lower Lane, at the junction of Lowerhouse Lane and East Lancashire Road, included a roundabout encircled by tracks, one of only a few examples in the UK. The constant procession of cars either terminating here or proceeding east towards the labour-intensive trading estates and factories at Gillmoss and Kirkby was supplemented at shift-change times by scores of heavily laden extras. Until early 1952 these had included the long, unnumbered Kirkby–Dingle route which ran just a couple of times a day — what a ride! The first view shows the city side of the roundabout; the land on the far right would later be occupied by Coronation Court, a 10-storey block of flats. In November 1955 'Liners' 909, outbound to Kirkby on route 19, and 889, inbound on route 13, cross as a solitary workman waits for the Austin A40 Somerset car to pass. The second view, recorded on 3 April 1954, shows 'Marks Bogie' No 867 near the end of its life. It had entered service in February 1936, four months before the first 'Streamliner'. The 70-seat domed-roof cars fell into two basic groups — the 'Marks Bogies' and the earlier, heavier (20-ton) 'Cabin' cars. The last 'Marks Bogies', known to crews as 'Pneumonia cars' because of the draughts whistling round platforms, were withdrawn in March 1955.
J. B. C. McCann

During the war the grass tracks were rapidly extended eastwards, reaching the city boundary in 1942, Hornhouse Lane in 1943 and finally the Royal Ordnance Factory at Kirkby (workforce 30,000) in 1944. This photograph was taken on 27 June 1954, approximately a year after a crossover had been installed here to cater for a new overspill housing development at Southdene (left). The terminus was located on the roadside reservation alongside the A580 East Lancashire Road (right). Trams continuing to Kirkby enjoyed a fast, uninterrupted mile-long run to the stop at Hornhouse Lane, which served the slab-like ICI Metals (later Yorkshire Metals) factory. The crew of car 166 are resting alongside the Bundy clock, used throughout the network to regulate timekeeping. On leaving Southdene the 19s reached Church Street by way of Walton Hall Avenue, Sleepers Hill and Shaw Street. After just 13 years, on 3 November 1956, this high-speed, semi-rural tramway was abandoned. Recent plans to incorporate parts into Merseytram line 1 have been dropped. *J. Soper / Leeds Historic Transport Society*

Contrasting with Kirkby's tower blocks was this charming sandstone bridge on rural Mill Lane. Since January 1965 the 15D had provided a direct link between the city and nearby Tower Hill Estate; this formed part of the massive Kirkby housing project, whereby thousands were rehoused as part of the slum clearances of the 1950s and '60s. Unfortunately there were few amenities, and the fare into town was seen as too expensive. 'Jumbo' 1194 (XKC 821K) belonged to the final batch of buses ordered by the Corporation but was not delivered until 1971. On these 80-seat Alexander-bodied Atlanteans the staircase was behind the driver and the centre exit door immediately aft of the front axle. *Photobus*

London Road was the principal exit for routes serving the northern and eastern suburbs. This lively scene was recorded at its junction with Lime Street (right) and Commutation Row (left). Most of the traffic in the foreground, including the L&G Fire Protection Morris Minor van, would have come up from the tunnel. In tram days there had been a 'grand union' — a double-track cross-junction with double-track linking curves on all four sides. At this time movements through the intersection were controlled from a special raised box by a policeman wearing white coat and gloves, to guarantee maximum visibility. On the right can be seen the awning of the Odeon, one of the city's once-numerous cinemas. London Road ceased to be a thriving commercial centre from August 1965, after the lower part was made one-way inbound; the re-routeing of all outbound buses proved disastrous for local businesses, and by the time two-way working was restored, in September 1983, many shops had closed. On the corner with Commutation Row was one of several branches of Burton, symbolising an area once home to many tailors and outfitters. The ornate cast-iron lamp-post remains today. *J. G. Parkinson / Online Transport Archive*

Left: Framed (left) by Woolworth and T. J. Hughes, another major city store, and Monument Place (right), 'Baby Grand' No 263 and Alexander-bodied Leyland PD2/20 L63 (NKD 663) of 1954 emerge from the narrow portion of London Road east of its junction with Pembroke Place. All the vehicles visible are on variations of the 10, which, together with other routes, provided an intensive service along the densely populated Kensington/Prescot Road corridor. Following conversion of the 10c to bus in June 1952 four cars provided a 20min weekday off-peak headway on the 10B until March 1955. No 263 survived until 1957, and L63 until 1969. During the summers of 1964 and 1965 the latter was one of several buses adapted for use on the service between Lime Street station and the Isle of Man ferries, the longitudinal seats at the rear of the lower saloon being temporarily replaced with luggage racks.
J. B. C. McCann

From December 1965 Monument Place (formerly Monument Square), in the fork of London Road and Pembroke Place, was the terminus for a new City Circle (later Cityride). Charging a flat fare of 3d (1.25p), this city-centre route, which was in no way a circle, was intended to counteract the downside of the various traffic-management schemes by offering better links between 'Shops & Stations'. The five dedicated double-deckers, painted in reversed livery and with fixed indicator displays, carried advertisements urging the public to 'Shop by Bus'. Four, including L164 (RKC 265), came from a batch of 30 Leyland PD2/Alexander 58-seaters with full-width bonnets, delivered during the winter of 1954/5. As the 'Circle' buses were operated from Garston garage much costly dead mileage was incurred. The service was withdrawn in September 1969. Although Monument Place is now pedestrianised many features remain recognisable. TJ's and the pub (to which the Bedford TK lorry is making deliveries) remain, although the post office has moved into the building next door and now shares this building with a café. Singing legend Frankie Vaughan was born a short distance to the north, in Kempston Street. *Peter Jackson*

The road markings in Daulby Street giving clear evidence of earlier traffic arrangements in the area, this view was recorded in September 1970, three months after buses using the eastern end of London Road were re-routed inbound via Daulby Street and Pembroke Place. The Majestic cinema (right) on the corner of Boundary Place had closed its doors, the whole area later being absorbed into the Royal Liverpool Hospital complex. Overlooked by the former Martin's Bank building (still standing today), an inbound 19A has just traversed the once busy junction at the foot of Prescot Street; another equally busy intersection lay a short distance away at Islington Square at the other end of Moss Street (background). Purchased for the final stages of the tram-replacement programme, L253 (VKB 709) was one of a batch of 35 Crossley-bodied Leyland PD2/20s, all of which had entered service by January 1957. Operating from Walton garage, they could often be found on former tram routes 19 and 44. Following delivery of the first Atlanteans the livery had become even more spartan, with elimination of the cream around the front of the vehicle. *A. F. Gahan*

Right: This evocative view shows the two faces of a city in transition. Representing the 1960s slogan 'City of Change and Challenge' is the new St John's Precinct Beacon; symbolising the past are streets like Brunswick Road, once home to substantial three-storey villas, the ground floors of which were later converted into shops. For over half a century this had been a busy commercial thoroughfare, but by the late 1950s properties were for sale or boarded up. Climbing up from Islington Square on 14 July 1971 is L57 (NKD 657), one of 60 exposed-radiator Leyland PD2/12s delivered in 1953 with 56-seat 8ft-wide 'Aurora'-style Weymann bodywork, the bulk of which passed to the PTE in 1969. Brunswick Road is now an extension of the Islington dual carriageway taking traffic out to the east of the city centre and is totally unrecognisable from the scene shown here. *A. F. Gahan*

Right: In October 1966 buses working in from West Derby Road and Everton Road were re-routed along Low Hill in lieu of Erskine Street. Double yellow lines had made their appearance when this view was recorded on 30 June 1972. Inbound on a peak-hour short-journey 14A, L204 (SKB 201), with Orion-style Weymann bodywork built to Liverpool specification, had been delivered for conversion of tram routes 19 and 44. Behind the bus are Grant Gardens and, close by, the Hippodrome cinema (formerly Hengler's Grand Circus, capacity 4,500). The pub at the top of Brunswick Road is 'Gregson's Well', one of two pubs across the road from each other with the same name, one of which was a notable venue for the city's thriving folk music scene and groups such as The Spinners. To the left of the two yellow Ford Transit vans is the Corner House Café, while to the right of the bus is Thistle House, occupied by builders' merchants Ferguson & Harvey. Some of these buildings can still be seen today. *A. F. Gahan*

Left: On 4 May 1970 L301 (VKB 757) approaches town at the junction of West Derby Road and Boaler Street, with Emmanuel Church (1867) in the fork. This junction has now disappeared, and Boaler Street is blocked off. Behind the church were the Olympia Theatre (later the Locarno Ballroom) and the Grafton Rooms. Immediately beyond this short stretch of surviving Victoriana, most of West Derby Road and Rocky Lane had, by this time, already been transformed into a dual carriageway. Overlooked by a faded Bent's public house, a knot of passengers look anxiously towards town. Despite a high level of service, buses were often full. On traditional open-platform vehicles a chain would stop people boarding and conductors gave three bells which told the driver not to stop. L301 was one of 30 Leyland PD2/30s delivered in 1957 with Crossley body frames; they should have been finished at Edge Lane, but after a period in store they were completed in 1961 by MCW. These 64-seaters had heaters and rear-facing seats at the front of the lower saloon. All 30 passed to the PTE in 1969. *A. F. Gahan*

Left: Action on the open section of Rocky Lane, with Newsham Park lake and gardens on the south side. Working into town on a peak-hour duty was veteran L396 (MKB 916) of 1952. Renumbered from L833 in 1966, this was one of 60 Leyland Titan PD2/12s with 8ft-wide 56-seat Weymann Aurora bodywork. The entire batch spent their working lives at the Green Lane/Carnegie Road group of garages. Withdrawals started in 1966. Photographed on 21 March 1967, L396 was among the last four to be withdrawn in 1969. It is in the drab unlined livery adopted after the introduction of the Atlanteans. Travelling towards Tuebrook is Atlantean L604 (604 KD), new in 1963. *A. F. Gahan*

This was the junction in Tuebrook at the east end of West Derby Road. In tram days the 11 had turned right into Green Lane; the 12 continued straight ahead on a central reservation towards West Derby, whilst the 29 turned left in front of the 1930s block of flats onto the Muirhead Avenue 'grass tracks'. Joining the mix was the outer-suburban route 49. For many years, with a few minor changes, the replacing buses followed similar route patterns. Colour views of this generation of early-postwar Leylands purchased for the tram-replacement programme are rare. No L448

(JKF 464) was one of 20 Titan PD2/1s delivered between December 1948 and February 1949 with constant-mesh gearboxes and, unusually for Liverpool, Leyland's standard five-bay bodywork, the Corporation generally preferring a four-bay design. Seen on 31 August 1967, shortly before it was withdrawn, the 56-seater was *en route* to the peak-hour queuing point in North John Street. This style of destination display was standard until the arrival of 8ft-wide vehicles. *A. F. Gahan*

This photograph was taken on 3 April 1954 — the final day of operation of routes 29 and 47. The latter was an industrial service linking Edge Lane with Muirhead Avenue East. *En route* to Edge Lane depot, having taken a full load of workers back to their homes, 'Baby Grand' No 263 stands outside the Carlton cinema, Tuebrook, waiting for the city-bound 29 to depart and for the duty inspector to give the 'all clear' to turn into Green Lane. The overhead skate activated the electric points.

Conversion of the 29 resulted in the closure of the ill-fated Green Lane depot, where fire had destroyed five trams in 1942 and 66 in 1947, the victims including 'Streamliners' and 'Baby Grands'. After conversion of the 29 a further 22 'Liners' would be sold to Glasgow, coincidentally to work that city's 29 (Milngavie–Broomhouse), following 24 sold the previous year. *J. B. C. McCann*

Having reached Muirhead Avenue East in 1938, tram lines were extended on roadside reservation to Lower Lane in 1943, allowing cars from the eastern and southern suburbs to reach the industrial complexes on the East Lancashire Road. Again seen on the last day of operation (3 April 1954), 'Baby Grand' No 216 carries an advert for Littlewoods, which, together with Vernons, made Liverpool the centre of the lucrative football-pools industry, both firms employing predominantly female labour. Each week pools agents went from house to house collecting coupons — and paying out winnings to a lucky few! The playing fields behind the fence have since been built on.
J. B. C. McCann

The first of two views featuring the Sheil Road Circular, numbered 26 in the clockwise direction from the city and 27 anti-clockwise. Trams had operated every three minutes on these 'outer circular' or 'belt' routes, which, owing to the preponderance of single track with passing loops, were the first to be converted from tram to bus in June 1948, reducing the journey time by roughly a quarter. Frequent and well-patronised, the 'circular' provided an invaluable inter-suburban link by travelling along or crossing over many other transport arteries. In tram days free transfers had been available between designated routes. Pictured working a 26 in Sheil Road on 19 September 1971 is L739 (CKF 739C), one of a batch of 60 Atlanteans delivered during the winter of 1965/6 which were slightly longer than earlier models and provided space for a tip-up conductor's seat at the front. Indicative of falling standards, the driver seems not to be wearing a uniform, and the 'via' blind is incorrectly set. The 26/27 circular would go OMO in July 1972. *A. F. Gahan*

The second view was taken on 1 October 1965 in Kensington, a short distance from the course of the first horse-drawn 'street railway', operated in 1861 from the then city boundary to Old Swan. Dating from 1958, L367 (WKF 223) came from the final batch of 25 open-platform Leyland PD2s to be delivered (although the 1957 vehicles stored until 1961 were the last to enter service). It was also part of the last group of Liverpool buses to have Crossley bodywork, the Stockport firm having supplied 346 bodies and frames between 1951 and 1958. In this case the driver's windscreen was flush with the full-width radiator grille. Among the shops on the left is one owned by local sweet manufacturer Barker & Dobson. *I. G. Holt*

Knotty Ash, spiritual home of tickling-sticks, Diddymen and the Jam Butty Mines, had been the meeting-point between the trams of the Corporation and the Liverpool & Prescot Light Railway, and at one time plans existed for goods trams to link the Docks with much of South Lancashire. At the end of World War 1 the worn-out single-track cross-country light railway was acquired by the Corporation, and when a four-mile stretch of the A57 was rebuilt in the 1920s it included a tramway reservation. Trams on inter-urban route 10 connected at Prescot with St Helens trams until 1936 and trolleybuses until 1949, when the 10 was converted to buses; it was also over these tracks that Liverpool's illuminated tram went on hire to towns such as Stockport and Ashton-under-Lyne (44 miles) between 1924 and 1934. This photograph shows 'Liner' No 907 inbound towards Old Swan on 5 March 1955. The original light railway had followed the road in the background, where a stub, reactivated during the war, was retained until 1949. On the right of the picture can be seen some of the hundreds of 'prefabs' that were built on open land to provide cheap housing for those displaced by the bombing. Knotty Ash said goodbye to its last trams, which used the tracks in the foreground, in September 1957 Ken Dodd and the Diddymen were 'discumknockerated'. *J. B. C. McCann*

Broad Green Road, a relatively lightly trafficked tree-lined thoroughfare linking Old Swan with Edge Lane Drive, was used by both the 61 and the 68, two outer-suburban orbital routes connecting Seaforth and Aigburth. Captured on 30 August 1970, Leyland Atlantean L621 (621 KD) is seen on the 61 via Walton, whilst Panther 1005 (FKF 884F) is on the 68 via West Derby. Both routes incorporated sections of longer-established services and carried heavy traffic, requiring peak-hour supplementary journeys starting from Old Swan. The photograph was taken shortly before the 61 was converted to OMO, in June 1971, the 68 having been amongst the first routes to be converted, in July 1968. *A. F. Gahan*

Pictured on route H16 to Elizabeth Road, Huyton, on a snowy day in the late 1960s, Crosville DLG897 (854 AFM) typifies the 352 low-floor half-cab Bristol LD Lodekkas delivered to the company during the 1950s, with either Bristol or Gardner engines. The ingenious design of the Lodekka permitted a central aisle on the upper deck within an overall vehicle height of about 13ft 5in, necessary because of the proliferation of low bridges across the company's operating area, and its introduction resulted in the rapid disappearance from the streets of older designs, with sunken offside gangway upstairs. Everything in this view in Bowring Park Road, including the former tramway reservation, would later be swept away to facilitate construction of the M62 motorway. *Peter Jackson*

Right and below right: Liverpool had led the way in the construction of modern reserved track tramways. These two views illustrate different aspects of the first section, opened in September 1914. Conceived by James A. Brodie, City Engineer from 1898 to 1926, the 'grass tracks' in the middle of spacious dual carriageways were part of an overall strategy for relocating people out of overcrowded inner-city dwellings. They would move into new spacious 'garden suburbs' with quality housing built on cheaply acquired land and served by swift, affordable electric tramways. Although towns such as Birmingham, Glasgow, Leeds, Sheffield and Sunderland followed suit, only Liverpool built up a substantial mileage, over a 30-year period, reaching a maximum of nearly 28 miles. Unfortunately the dual carriageways were not always continuous; for example, breaks occurred for narrow bridges, as in the first view, over the original Liverpool & Manchester Railway, with Broad Green station in the background. This entire streetscape is now lost beneath the start of the M62, the site of the Lucas factory (right) now being occupied by housing and the Turnpike Tavern. The second view shows Edge Lane Drive, most of which remains unchanged today. It was on the 'grass tracks' that the 'Streamliners', with their four 40hp motors, are said to have frequently exceeded 55mph. This historic first section remained in use until 14 September 1957. *A. P. Tatt; Ray DeGroote*

Repainted in reversed livery as the official last tram, 'Baby Grand' No 293 ran in service thus from 8 to 14 September 1957. During this final week all tram conductors carried a range of souvenir Bell Punch tickets, including workmen's returns, set to disappear with the passing of the trams. Also going was that thrifty Liverpool institution, the 'child's penny return'; available during school holidays for the price of 1d (0.4p), this enabled children from all backgrounds to explore their city and its tramway. Watched by dejected enthusiasts, No 293 approaches Edge Lane depot (right) after making the last public service trip to Bowring Park (6A) on Saturday 14 September; later it would bring up the rear of the final procession. On 7 May 1958 it again left Edge Lane but this time for a streetcar museum in the USA. It is still there today with its inscription '1897 LIVERPOOL'S LAST TRAM 1957'. *J. B. C. McCann*

For most of 1956 the remaining 31 'Liners' had worked mostly peak-hour and extra duties on routes 6, 6A and 40 for the combined wokforces at Littlewoods, Meccano, Crawfords Biscuits and the Automated Telephone Co. With the 5½-day week still in force their final runs took place during the early afternoon of Saturday 3 November 1956. Captured on a short working to Clayton Square, No 158 was one of 25 'Streamliners' rehabilitated only the previous year, when leaks were sealed, seats repaired and flooring and wiring renewed. Just discernible in the background (right) is the Edge Lane works and depot complex, opened in 1928 and destined to be demolished in 1997; originally employing 900, it had been self-sufficient, building hundreds of modern trams and assembling scores of bus bodies. However, for many years it had not been cost-effective, making closure inevitable. The women on the right have congregated outside Littlewoods Pools' coupon-sorting centre, an art-deco building which survives today but in other usage. *M. Jenkins / E. C. Bennett / Online Transport Archive*

Several photographs in this book were taken by one-time members of the Liverpool University Public Transport Society (LUPTS), and — not surprisingly — include some around the University. In the first view the advertisement for *The Times* is something of a giveaway. The hoardings at the top of Brownlow Hill are masking derelict land later occupied by the Electrical Engineering Department, as seen in the second view. In fact, most of this area has now been consumed by the ever-expanding university, which started life in a former lunatic asylum before becoming fully independent in 1903. The term 'red brick', used to describe universities originating in the late 19th and early 20th century, was coined by a Liverpool professor based on the preponderance of red brick and terracotta used in construction of the Victoria Building (1892), with its Jubilee Tower and clock. More prosaically, A475 (GKF 74) was one of 42 AEC Regent IIs with 56-seat Weymann bodywork completed at Edge Lane. On entering service in February 1947 it carried no fleet number, becoming A275 in May and A475 in 1957. Seen working back to depot after the morning peak, when less-congested streets were often used, it survived only a few more months after the photograph was taken, on 8 February 1963. In the second view, recorded on 17 May 1970, a Bedford CA ice-cream van pursues an unpainted MCW-bodied Regent V, A230 (VKB 828) of 1959. On the right is part of an extensive Roman Catholic site that includes all that was built of Sir Edwin Lutyens' design for one of the largest cathedrals in the world (never completed, due to rising costs), as well as the present cathedral, consecrated in 1967. The site had previously been occupied by an 18th-century workhouse.
G. D. Smith; A. F. Gahan

Left: Brownlow Hill carried the last new central-area section of tramway, opened in December 1936. At the city end was a short length of single track controlled by colour-light signals activated by a skate in the overhead. Taken in July 1957, the first of two photographs at this location features inbound 'Baby Grand' No 201 passing Parry's bookshop — frequented by generations of students — and a Reece's confectioners. Later, when this road was widened, little Mary Ann Street, behind the Double Diamond hoarding, disappeared completely, as did the war-damaged area in front, all swallowed up by a car park. *A. P. Tatt*

Right: In the second view, recorded on 30 July 1955, 'Liner' No 906 on an outbound 40 stands just short of the single track. In the absence of external mirrors the driver keeps an eye on those boarding — especially the man with his arm in a sling. To the right is the ballroom and garage entrance of the Adelphi Hotel (1914) — once *the* place to stay (and subsequently the star of its own TV series). Rising phoenix-like behind 906 is the postwar building of Lewis's, a proud Liverpool firm since 1856. The prewar Lewis's had once been the largest store in the North of England. In the days before parking meters and yellow lines motorists parked wherever they fancied — even if it involved facing in the wrong direction on corners (right). Among the cars lined up herringbone-fashion on Mount Pleasant (left) are a couple of Ford Populars and a prewar Austin Cambridge and Hillman Minx, whilst nosing out carefully to overtake the tram is a Humber Hawk.
D. G. Clarke

In the south of the city Rathbone Road, Wavertree, which had been served by Corporation buses since 1914, ran close to one of the most complex railway sites in the world. For many years residents in this well-maintained terrace were in earshot of activity at Edge Hill locomotive shed as well as at the nearby gridiron, a massive gravity-operated marshalling yard, open round the clock, handling traffic to and from the docks. The former railway site is now partially occupied by Wavertree Technology Park. Rathbone Road was (and still is) served by orbital route 60. On 27 August 1970 one of the last AEC Regent IIIs to be delivered (in early 1955), Crossley-bodied A94 (NKD 594), heads towards Picton Road on a 60B short-working. *A. F. Gahan*

The major Crosville corridor to and from the city included the High Street in Wavertree, once an ancient village settlement. Seen just east of Wavertree (or Picton) Clock Tower, Crosville CMG361 (201 KFM) heads along Childwall Road, outbound to Prescot via Whiston Hospital on the hourly H12 service. When new in 1958 this vehicle, an ECW-bodied Bristol MW, would have operated Crosville's flagship services to London, but by the time this picture was taken *c*1970 it had largely been relegated to local services. Later still it would be fully downgraded as a service bus, losing its coach seats, being fitted with an electrically operated door and equipped for OMO, in which guise it was to last until 1976. The clock tower had formerly overlooked an important tramway junction, including a short extension opened to Childwall Five Ways as late as 1936. When the 99 buses replaced the 49 trams in September 1952 the Church Road (left) and Mill Lane (right) tracks were retained, providing a link between Garston depot and Edge Lane works. They were last used in June 1953. *Peter Jackson*

A crisp winter's day in pleasant suburban surroundings in Thingwall Road, Wavertree, with the Electric Supply Company social club in the background. Delivered in September 1957 to replace the last of the trams, A203 (VKB 801) was an AEC Regent V with an MCW body frame completed at Edge Lane. All Regent Vs delivered after November 1956 had 62-seat Orion-style bodies with rear-facing seats at the front of the lower saloon and Liverpool-designed radiator grilles.

In PTE days the attractive city coat of arms displayed on buses was replaced by the more functional 'Catherine Wheel'. Operation of the 76, linking the city to Broad Green via Wavertree, passed from the PTE to Crosville in October 1973. It was to remain crew-operated until the withdrawal of the last Lodekkas in 1981.
Peter Jackson

The revolutionary, rear-engined Leyland Atlantean had a major impact on bus operation in the city over four decades. The Corporation's first was E2 (372 BKA), which arrived in December 1959 for evaluation. The experiment was a success, and subsequently large orders were placed, albeit for vehicles with a more stylish design of bodywork. Merseyside PTE kept faith with the Atlantean, and deliveries continued almost without break until September 1984. Seen c1972 in Thingwall Road, Wavertree, E2 remained crew-operated after passing to the PTE; finally sold in January 1978, it served as a mobile home before being secured for preservation. The last Atlanteans would not depart the streets of Liverpool until 2001. *Peter Jackson*

Photographed in May 1971, a pair of Leyland Panthers, 1057 (FKF 936G) leading, head along Smithdown Road towards its junction with Ullet Road. The 5 and 46 were among the handful of routes converted to OMO in the dying days of the Corporation. Some 110 Panthers, with dual-door, 47-seat MCW bodywork, were bought in 1968/9 to facilitate the OMO programme before the use of double-deck one-man vehicles was legalised. However, they were not particularly successful, and large-scale withdrawals began as early as 1977. Trams on the Garston circle had last operated along Smithdown Road in June 1953. This part of Smithdown Road, with its houses of Welsh yellow brick, is almost unchanged today. *Alan Atkinson*

Right: Completing the trio of experimental vehicles bought in 1959 to decide future vehicle policy was E1 (371 BKA), a 30ft AEC Regent V with full-fronted, 72-seat Park Royal body complete with power-operated forward entrance. Fitted with heaters (very welcome on a wintry day), the latest engine design and the standard AEC grille, it entered service in August of that year and by 1960 had worked from every garage except Prince Alfred Road. Photographed on 2 February 1963 just south of Penny Lane, it was proceeding along Allerton Road on tram-replacement route 4. No E1 proved to be the final new Regent to be acquired by the Corporation, the last of a long line going back to 1935. After passing to Merseyside PTE in 1969 it saw little regular service before joining the driver-training fleet for a short spell, after which it was sold in 1974. Now preserved, it belongs to the Merseyside Transport Trust, which has built up a large, representative selection of Liverpool Corporation vehicles. *G. D. Smith*

Right: Liverpool is renowned for the range and variety of its public parks, the 'green lungs' essential for any major industrial city. One of the most impressive is Calderstones Park, once the home of a wealthy merchant. Also in part a Botanic Garden, it was served by the Corporation's first bus route (1911), a short feeder service connecting the tram terminus in Menlove Avenue with Woolton, eventually reached by trams in 1924. In this view, dated 16 October 1971, inbound Panther 1064 (FKF 943G) passes the park on the right and the former tramway central reservation, abandoned in 1949, on the left. The yellow sticker on the front signified that the vehicle was fitted with a Bus Economy Ticket (BET) machine. The BET was a short-lived stored-value ticket, whereby passengers received a discount by paying for 10 journeys in advance. The distinctive cream OMO livery was abandoned after delivery of the Panthers and 25 Bristol REs, and the majority were subsequently repainted in the predominantly green livery. The last Panthers would be withdrawn by the PTE in 1981. *A. F. Gahan*

With its blinds already changed to show '33 PIER HEAD' No 937 approaches Garston in May 1951. When the reservation along Horrocks Avenue opened on 4 July 1939 it provided a vital link between Allerton and Garston and led to a major route reorganisation, some of the trams arriving at Garston via Aigburth continuing back to town via Allerton and *vice versa*. However, the planned extensions to Speke never materialised, and, despite costly postwar renewal of several lengthy sections of track, trams on the Garston 'Circle' were replaced by buses from 7 June 1953. As a result all but one of the 25 'Liners', on Maley & Taunton swing-link trucks,

were sold to Glasgow, for £500 each. They were followed a year later by a further 22 'Liners', this time on a mix of EMB 'HR2' and lightweight trucks. They enjoyed relatively short lives in their new home, the last example being withdrawn in June 1960. Fortunately, thanks to the efforts of early members of the Liverpool University Public Transport Society, one 'Liner' (869) was preserved and now resides at the National Tramway Museum at Crich, Derbyshire.
W. J. Wyse / LRTA London Region

The frontage of the single-span 1940 extension, built on the east wall of the original Garston depot (1910) is visible in this view of No 947 standing on the Speke Road reservation in May 1951. Route 33 reached town by way of Aigburth and Dingle. Mounted on EMB lightweight trucks, this car, along with many other 'Liners', was to have its body reconstructed in the early 1950s. Garston was home to hundreds of workers employed on the local dock estate (1876-1909), developed by the London & North Western Railway for handling bulk cargoes including coal, bananas and timber. Nowadays part of Associated British Ports, the docks are still open but are no longer rail-connected. *W. J. Wyse / LRTA London Region*

Above: Setting for the TV sitcom *Bread* and birthplace of local luminaries Ringo Starr and John Gregson, Dingle was a densely populated area close to the once thriving South Docks. It was also an early transport hub, served by the Overhead Railway's underground terminus in Park Road (1896) and by the first electric trams (1898), when a substantial new depot was built fronting onto this wide expanse of roadway. This became a hive of activity, with many routes, including peak-hour extras, either passing through or terminating. In this view one of the first 'tin-fronted' AECs waits to work a 'short turn' into the city. Purchased for conversion of the Garston routes in June 1953, A4 (NKD 504) was one of 100 AEC Regent IIIs delivered 1953-5 which featured a full-width radiator grille designed by the Corporation. All but two had Crossley 8ft-wide 56-seat bodies like the one shown here. No A4 survived long enough to pass to the PTE, with which it served, latterly as a driver-training bus, until 1973. Behind Toxteth Congregational Church (since demolished) are Princes Park and Sefton Park, each with splendid older dwellings. *Alan Murray-Rust*

Right: Dingle was the southern terminus of the long-established route 3, on which buses replaced trams in 1948 and which was crew-operated until May 1970. In this view, recorded on 14 June 1969, A149 (SKB 149), an open-platform Regent V of 1956, has just arrived, whilst L874 (FKF 874E), a 1967 Atlantean, is about to pass the big Gaumont cinema on Park Road at the start of its cross-city run to Walton via Lime Street. Built as single-door buses, the last 50 Atlanteans (L830-79) were rebuilt by Pennine Coachcraft when just two years old, the conversion including a central staircase, a centre exit, a two-piece destination display and OMO equipment. Behind A149 can be seen the gables of Dingle depot, closed to trams in 1951 and buses in 1965. When it was demolished in July 1993 a pair of mosaics featuring the Liver Bird and the words 'ELECTRIC TRAMWAYS' were rescued for preservation. The housing estate built on the site includes street names with strong tramway connections — Maley (tramcar trucks) and Mallins (a former tramways manager). In the background a Regent Oil Atkinson articulated tanker turns into Aigburth Road. *Alan Murray-Rust*

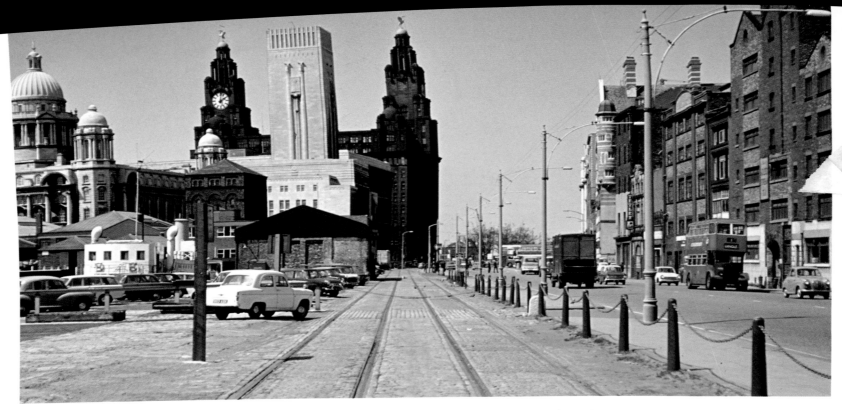

Our journey around the streets of Liverpool brings us back almost to Pier Head, this time approaching it from the south. The LOR has gone, but the MDHB 'main line' remains. Regular movements over this latter ceased in 1961; the last train trundled along, bell clanging, red-flag man walking in front, some 10 years later. This portion of the Dock Road is known as Strand Street. For years the Liverpool waterfront was known as 'the cast-iron shore', owing to the use of cast-iron in much of the warehouse construction, including the incomparable Albert Dock (1846). Designed by Dock Engineer Jesse Hartley, this Grade I-listed structure was the first enclosed dock warehouse complex and is now a major tourist attraction. Two other early nearby docks, Canning and Salthouse, also survive. However, like too much of Liverpool's extraordinary industrial heritage, the warehouses behind the AEC Regent III in this May 1966 view would be torn down. Other architectural features include the dome of the Dock Board building and, framed by the twin towers of the Liver Building, the white stone ventilator shaft (1934) for the first Mersey road tunnel and the brick-built Mersey Railway pumping station (1886).
Peter J. Davies

Back cover: The Prescot inter-urban tramway was cut back to Longview Lane in 1949 and to Pagemoss in 1952, the last mile between Pagemoss and Pilch Lane surviving until September 1957. To cater for all the trams terminating at Pagemoss there was a turning-circle and a double-track siding as well as a crossover on the 'main line' which had continued eastwards to Prescot. Different stops separated those going directly into town from those going 'the posh way' via Edge Lane. The shopping parade on the left typified the ribbon development that followed reconstruction of the A57 in the 1920s and provided local amenities for the hundreds of people living in this immediate area. The bus (right) approaching the Eagle & Child public house was one of the first generation of postwar Leyland PD2/1s with 56-seat bodywork built by the Wakefield firm of Charles Roberts (no relation to the author!). *J. B. C. McCann*